Shrink your WORRIES

SHRINK YOUR WORRIES

Copyright © Summersdale Publishers Ltd, 2024

An Hachette UK Company
www.hachette.co.uk

Vie Books, an imprint of Summersdale Publishers Ltd
Part of Octopus Publishing Group Limited
Carmelite House
50 Victoria Embankment
LONDON
EC4Y 0DZ
UK

www.summersdale.com

Printed and bound in Poland

ISBN: 978-1-83799-172-3

Substantial discounts on bulk quantities of Summersdale books are available to corporations, professional associations and other organizations. For details contact general enquiries: telephone: +44 (0) 1243 771107 or email: enquiries@summersdale.com.

Shrink Your Worries

WORRIES

A Child's Guide to Overcoming Anxiety

POPPY O'NEILL

Contents

Foreword

By Amanda Ashman-Wymbs, Counsellor and Psychotherapist, registered and accredited by the British Association for Counselling and Psychotherapy

After working with young people therapeutically for many years and having raised two daughters, it is evident that finding ways to help children manage and understand anxiety is greatly needed. Living in today's fast-paced society, children are often out of sync with their natural calm, and learning how to work with the thoughts and feelings that come from tension, stress and fear is invaluable.

Shrink Your Worries by Poppy O'Neill is a wonderful little workbook aimed at 7–11-year-olds to help support them in their journey towards feeling calmer, braver and less anxious. Written in an easy-to-understand and friendly way, it assists the child in learning how to recognize signs of anxiety in the mind and body, as well as boosting their emotional understanding and literacy skills. As the child works through this book, they are supported in learning to identify what their worries are, and are offered ideas and techniques to help put these into perspective and overcome them.

There is emphasis on talking with a trusted grown-up, doing breathing exercises, making affirmations for themselves, identifying errors in their thinking, taking care of the mind and body through diet and sleep, and learning to understand the difference between facts and opinions. They are also encouraged to take small, guided steps, one at a time, towards growing their bravery and learning how to shrink the fears which may be limiting their lives.

This is a gem of a book to help support children who worry.

Introduction:
A guide for parents and carers

Created using techniques used by child psychologists and therapists, *Shrink Your Worries* is a practical guide for children to help them understand and manage feelings of anxiety.

Anxiety is a healthy human emotion that everybody feels to some extent. In fact, it's a very useful feeling that humans have evolved in order to keep us safe. Thousands of years ago the sensation of anxiety acted as an early warning signal of danger from wild animals or other threats. While the modern world is very different, these instincts are still a strong part of how we perceive our surroundings.

While everybody experiences anxiety and worries about relatively big and small things, your child might seem more prone to anxiety than others their age. It can feel like no matter how much you reassure them, that underlying sense of unease doesn't shift. The thing about anxiety is, like any emotion, it doesn't always follow logic. While we can convince our thinking minds that there is nothing threatening our safety, our emotional minds need a different approach.

This book is aimed at children aged 7–11, an age when it can feel like there's a lot to worry about. School and friendships take on a new seriousness, and awareness of others and the wider world can weigh heavy on young minds. No wonder it can be an anxious time.

Signs of anxiety

Anxiety can present itself in unexpected ways. It's not always how we might picture a worried child. Anxiety can come out as apathy, anger and criticism, and children often work hard to conceal their feelings in an effort not to upset those around them.

While some level of anxiety is normal and healthy for every child, look out for these signs that they may need extra support in dealing with and regulating their feelings of anxiety:

- They are very critical of themselves or others

- They seem unable to cope with everyday challenges

- They find it hard to concentrate

- They have trouble sleeping or eating properly

- They are prone to angry outbursts

- They experience intrusive, unwanted thoughts that they struggle to get out of their head

- They worry excessively that bad things are going to happen

- They avoid everyday activities such as going to school, seeing friends or going out in public

- They seek constant reassurance

While you may feel concerned about your child's expressions of anxiety, stay calm – you've got this. As parents and carers you are uniquely placed to support and influence your child's mental and emotional well-being simply by remaining a calm, steady presence in their lives.

Remember, anxieties can be difficult for children to talk about: there's no perfect thing you can say. Simply beginning a conversation is very powerful – this book is here to help you start.

Talking to your child about anxiety

When anxiety is getting in the way of your child enjoying their life, it can be tempting to either brush off their worries with logic ("You'll be fine, there's nothing to worry about.") or, at the other extreme, shield them completely from what's concerning them.

The way we can best help children overcome anxiety lies somewhere in the middle of these two approaches. As parents, we know our children better than anyone, and that knowledge enables us to strike a balance between taking our children's emotions seriously and gently challenging them to face their fears.

We can validate our children's emotions, showing them we understand how they are feeling, without confirming their fears. For example, if your child is worried about going to a birthday party, you could validate them by saying something like: "Something about this party feels worrying for you. Parties can be overwhelming, I get it!"

Showing understanding in this way will help your child relax, and from there you can explore solutions to help them feel braver and more comfortable.

Getting started

Let your child know that there's no rush to work through the chapters in this book. Allow them to go at their own pace and do the activities on their own – this will encourage your child's independence, as you are showing them that you trust them to have a go at challenges by themselves. At the same time, let them know that you're on hand to talk through anything they want to show you or ask you about.

The activities in this book are designed to get kids thinking about their minds and emotions, and how they deal with worries – while giving them the tools needed to recognize and manage anxiety.

Show your child that you take their worries seriously, even if they strike you as unrealistic – the emotion underneath is very real. Support your child to learn new habits and deal with their problems independently, and watch their confidence grow.

If you have any serious concerns about your child's mental health, your doctor is the best person to turn to for further advice.

Welcome to Shrink Your Worries

Welcome to *Shrink Your Worries,* a great guide for dealing with anxiety and the thoughts and feelings that come along with it. If you're reading this, you probably get worried sometimes. The truth is, everybody does – even if they don't show it on the outside. This fact doesn't make anxiety go away, but it can help to know you're not alone.

In this book you'll find lots of information and fun activities to help you learn about how anxiety works, what you can do about it, plus useful tricks and tools for shrinking your worries down to size. You might even learn some new things about your own mind and emotions along the way too.

How to use this book: A guide for children

This book is for you if you often…

☆ Feel nervous, worried or afraid

☆ Feel scared even when there isn't any real danger

☆ Find it difficult to talk about how you feel

☆ Get scary thoughts stuck in your head

☆ Don't want to leave your parents or carer because you are worried

☆ Feel tired or ill because of worrying

☆ Miss out on fun activities because of worrying

If that sounds like you (maybe a lot of the time, or maybe only sometimes), this book is jam-packed with activities and advice to help shrink your worries, feel braver and become more confident.

There's no rush, you can read through this book as quickly as you like, or read a bit and come back to it later.

If you get stuck, or want to talk about anything you see in this book, you can ask a trusted grown-up for help, or just for them to listen. That grown-up could be your mum or dad, your carer, one of your teachers, an aunt or uncle – or any adult that you know well and feel comfortable talking to about your feelings.

Meet the *Shrink Your Worries* gang!

On the pages of this book you'll find kids from the *Shrink Your Worries* gang to guide you through the activities, learning how to handle challenges and grow their bravery alongside you.

Part 1:
Anxiety explained

We all know what it feels like to worry, but what exactly is anxiety and why do we feel it? In this chapter we'll find out answers to these questions and more.

Activity: Growing bravery

We all feel worried and anxious sometimes. The trick to overcoming anxiety is to shrink your worries and grow your bravery so that your bravery becomes bigger than your worries. Bravery acts like a shield to help us feel able to do challenging things even when we feel worried or anxious.

Can you decorate this shield to represent your bravery? You could draw gemstones, your name and anything else that helps you feel brave, and use colours – like gold and silver – that stand for strength.

Some people think that being brave means not feeling scared or worried at all, but that's not true! True bravery means feeling anxious, scared or worried and acting with courage anyway.

Part 1: Anxiety explained

What are emotions?

Human beings have lots of different emotions. Scientists are still learning exactly what emotions are, but what we do know about them is that we experience them as sensations in our bodies, and that they have a big effect on the thoughts in our minds and the way we act.

The emotions we feel are always changing. We might wake up feeling worried, and by breakfast time feel excited for the day – or the other way around. Sometimes emotions change because of the things going on around us, and sometimes they change because of our thoughts. Here are some more facts about emotions.

- Emotions can feel small and quiet or big and loud. Some can feel nice, and some feel uncomfortable or bad.

- Everyone has feelings, and you can't always tell what someone's feeling from looking at them.

- When you are feeling an emotion, it can sometimes seem like the emotion is taking over your whole body, which can feel quite scary.

- It's OK to feel whatever you are feeling, and you are never bad or naughty for feeling an emotion.

Part I: Anxiety explained

We give names to the different ways we feel inside so we can talk about them with others. Think about what colour each emotion would be if they were colours and use that colour to shade in the bubbles.

Everybody feels emotions in their own unique way, so there are no wrong answers here – you are the expert on how it feels to be you.

Can you think of any more? Write and colour in some other emotions in these bubbles.

How do you feel?

Each day, we feel lots of different emotions and sensations in our bodies. How do you feel right now? Write and draw as many feelings as you like. E.g. calm, sad, happy, worried, shy, proud...

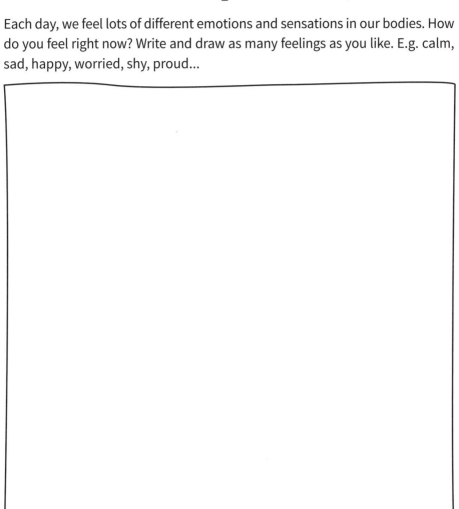

Noticing our emotions is an important part of understanding them. Keep reading to find out more about why we feel emotions.

Why do we feel anxious?

Anxiety is the feeling you get when something feels unsafe, or not quite right. In your body, it might feel like a tummy ache, a tightness in your chest, a heavy heart or something else. When we get this feeling that something's wrong, our brains sometimes start to come up with stories to explain why we feel this way. The stories our brains come up with are our worried thoughts. Here's Seamus's experience with worry and anxiety.

Seamus had a bad day at school yesterday. He fell over in the playground and none of his friends were nearby to help him. One child laughed at him, and Seamus felt embarrassed. A teacher came over to help and put a plaster on his cut knee.

Today, Seamus feels anxious when it's time to get ready for school. His brain gets to work coming up with worried thoughts:

Part I: Anxiety explained

Can you see how Seamus's brain is taking a memory from the past and using it to try and predict the future? When Seamus fell on the playground, his body *and* his feelings got hurt. Seamus's brain is doing its best to keep Seamus safe from that happening again.

Anxiety is just one of the emotions humans feel, and it's normal! In fact, it's a really important emotion that can keep you safe and help you make sensible choices. Humans evolved to feel scared and nervous to keep us safe from danger.

In the Stone Age, this meant watching out for sabre-toothed tigers…

Today, even though we aren't in danger from sabre-toothed tigers anymore, anxiety reminds us to be careful in the same way.

Sometimes it's helpful – like when we're near a hot cup of tea or walking across a wobbly log, anxiety helps us take extra care.

Other times, it's not so helpful – like for Seamus. Just because he had a bad experience one day, doesn't mean that going into school is dangerous. But anxiety can make it feel that way.

I am brave

Activity: How does Rebekah feel?

Rebekah's class is having a maths lesson. The teacher has explained what to do and written some questions on the board. But Rebekah doesn't understand. She looks around – her classmates are writing in their books, it looks like they do understand.

How do you think Rebekah feels? What might she be thinking? Write your ideas here:

_____

_____

_____

_____

_____

_____

Great answers! When it seems like we're the odd one out it can feel very difficult to ask for help. Rebekah might be having anxious thoughts about what her classmates or teacher will think. It will take bravery for Rebekah to ask for help.

What does anxiety feel like?

We feel anxious when we feel a mixture of worried, nervous and afraid. We can feel anxiety all over our bodies:

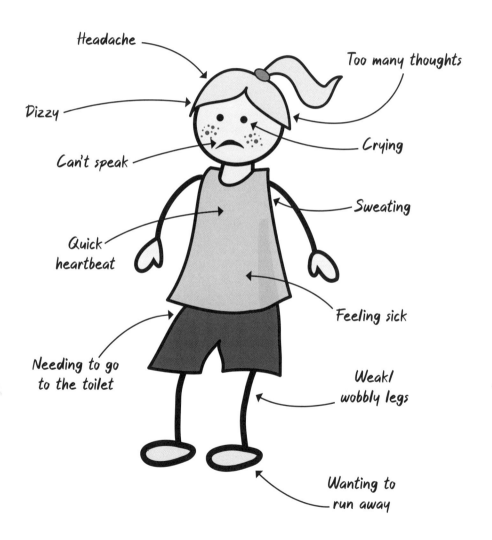

How do we worry?

There are lots of different kinds of anxiety…

- Some children feel very anxious about something in particular

- Some children feel anxious in certain situations

- Some children feel a bit anxious almost all the time, with lots of small worries that seem to fill up their minds

- Some children feel anxious about being away from their parents, or about meeting new people

- Some children feel anxious that bad things will happen to them or to people they love

- Some children feel they need to check or organize things because they think something bad will happen if they don't

- Some children feel anxious when unexpected things happen or their routine changes

We all feel anxious sometimes, in our own unique way. However you feel is OK, and you're not alone with your worries and feelings.

I belong here

Activity: All sorts of worry

Everyone feels worried or anxious about different things. There might be one thing that makes you feel anxious, or there might be many things. Here are just two examples:

Ibrahim feels anxious in his swimming lessons. There's something about the noise, the water and all the other children splashing that makes his body feel tense. It gets really hard for Ibrahim to speak when he feels anxious like this. He feels like he's frozen to the spot at the side of the pool.

Julia feels afraid of the dark. Even with the landing light on outside her door, the shadows in her room look frightening to her and she finds it really difficult to fall asleep at night. Sometimes she comes up with reasons to go downstairs, like needing a drink or to check something.

When do you feel anxious? It might be in a certain lesson or place, like Ibrahim; or perhaps it's a time of day, like Julia. Write or draw as many ideas as you like here:

How do you act when you are feeling anxious? For example, Ibrahim feels frozen to the spot and stays very still. Julia finds reasons to go out of her bedroom. Write or draw as many ideas as you like here:

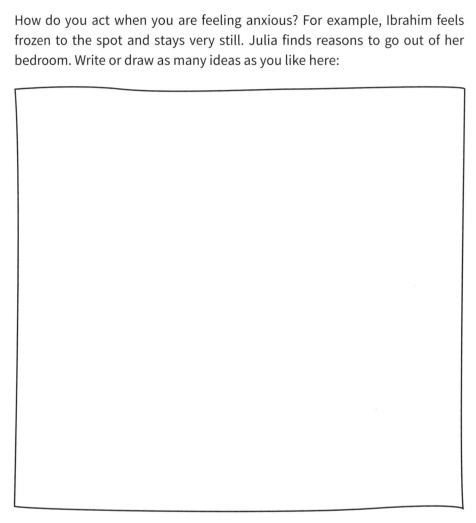

Sometimes, when we feel anxious, we act in ways that make us feel better for a little while – like putting off learning a new skill or hiding our true feelings – but that won't help change how we feel about that situation. Because we feel the same about the situation, our anxious thoughts will come back just the same next time. Later in this book we'll look at ways we can shrink our worries by thinking and acting in ways that build our bravery.

When anxiety feels overwhelming

Sometimes anxiety can feel so big that we feel our body is out of control. When this happens, our breathing gets really fast. We might feel dizzy, hot or sick, and our heart might beat faster.

Even when it feels big, horrible and scary, anxiety can't hurt you. When you feel very very anxious, there are things you can do to help you cope while it passes:

1. Ask for help from someone close by – you might want them to sit next to you, hug you or take deep breaths with you. If there's no one around, remember you can get through this feeling by yourself too.

2. Close your eyes.

3. Remember that the big feeling will end soon, and that it can't hurt you.

4. Think about your breathing. Count to five as you take a deep breath, then let it out slowly: 1, 2, 3, 4, 5.

5. Once the feeling has passed, you might feel tired or thirsty. Don't rush, take a moment to relax and see what your body needs.

Later in this book we'll look at lots of different ways to calm big feelings of anxiety.

I can take a deep breath

Part 2: Shrinking worries

Feelings of anxiety can be hard to deal with. They get in the way of making friends, having fun and relaxing! In this chapter you'll find lots of ideas for shrinking your worries, so you can find your bravery and get on with your day.

How do we shrink worries?

Worries and anxiety are our bodies telling us there might be danger. Remember that we can feel worry and anxiety even when we're safe. The way to shrink feelings of anxiety and worried thoughts is to grow feelings of safety and comfort.

We can do this in many ways:

- Doing things that help us feel safe, like having a cuddle or watching a funny film
- Sharing our worries with someone kind and understanding
- Changing how we think about ourselves and our emotions
- Going to our favourite outdoors space and enjoying the connection we feel with nature

When we take action to grow our feelings of safety, our worries start to shrink. When our worries shrink, we can grow our bravery and challenge ourselves. Keep reading for lots of ideas to help shrink your worries!

Talking to a trusted grown-up

Talking about how you are feeling and what's on your mind is a very powerful and important part of shrinking your worries. Often, when we feel anxious, we can feel worried about telling anybody or even about saying the worry out loud.

Talking about your worries and anxious feelings takes bravery, so when you share your worries, it makes sense to share them with someone you know and trust.

How to spot a trusted grown-up

☆ You know them already

☆ You feel safe and calm around them

☆ They show respect and kindness in their actions

☆ They are good at listening

A trusted grown-up might be a parent, carer, teacher, aunt, uncle or any grown-up you know.

Who could be your trusted grown-up? Write their name here:

Activity: Wriggle your worries out

Anxiety can make our bodies freeze up and feel very tense. Moving our bodies helps let the tension and anxious feelings out. Moving our bodies in a playful way sends the message to our brains that we are safe and there's no need to worry.

Try these anxiety-shrinking movements:

Do five tuck jumps

Drum on your knees

Wriggle like a jelly

Dance in a circle

Put your arms in the air and sway side to side

Sit on a chair and bounce your heels up and down

When you move your body in a wriggly, jiggly way, your movements actually help to calm down the part of your brain in charge of anxiety. It's called the amygdala and is found right above the top of your spine.

I feel safe and strong

Feeling worried about feeling worried

When we see someone else having big feelings, it can make us feel emotions too. For example, if your friend is excited about their new school bag, you might feel happy or excited with them – you might also feel jealous, bored, angry... we're all different.

Some of the time, it can feel scary to show our emotions to others, because we're worried that they might get upset, show us anger or even laugh at us. It's often this worry about how others might react that makes us want to keep our feelings inside.

It's like adding another layer of worry onto your worry cake!

When we have a trusted grown-up we can share our worries with, we can stop adding layers to our worry cakes.

Quick calmers

Here are some quick tricks you can do anywhere to help yourself feel calmer.

- ✧ Spell your name backwards
- ✧ Think about the soles of your feet – what can you feel?
- ✧ Breathe deeply, filling your lungs with fresh oxygen
- ✧ Shut your eyes and imagine wearing a lovely warm, snuggly coat
- ✧ Take a moment to look at all four corners of the room you're in
- ✧ Open your mouth as wide as you can
- ✧ Give yourself a cuddle
- ✧ Stretch up to the ceiling and then shake it out
- ✧ Drink a glass of water
- ✧ Try to balance on one foot

The anxiety hill

When anxiety starts to build inside you, it can feel really scary. Understanding how a feeling of anxiety happens can help you shrink that scary feeling. We usually experience anxiety in the shape of a hill, like this:

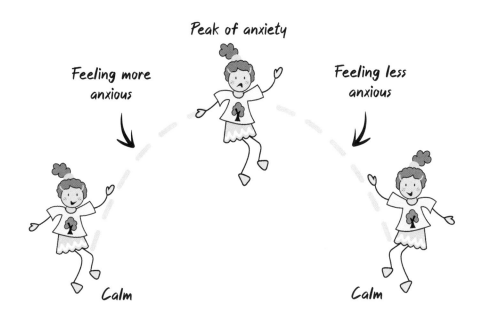

If you feel your anxiety starting to grow bigger, imagine this picture: the top of the hill is the point when you feel most anxious. If we get caught up in anxious thoughts, it can take longer to feel calm again, so try to breathe and let the feeling pass.

Once the feeling reaches the top of the hill it's important to know that it will not last for a long time and it will go back down the other side. Soon you will feel calmer and calmer.

Activity: Belly breathing

Here's a deep breathing activity to help calm anxiety. Taking deep, slow breaths brings extra oxygen into our bodies and helps grow feelings of safety so worries can shrink.

Here's how to belly breathe:

1. Find a soft, not too heavy object that will fit on your belly – teddies, small cushions and books are ideal.

2. Lie down somewhere comfortable.

3. Place the object on your belly.

4. Take a deep breath, concentrating on moving the air down into your belly.

5. Watch as your belly grows rounder and bigger, lifting the object up.

6. Breathe out slowly and steadily, so the object sinks down again.

7. Go slowly so the object doesn't fall off!

8. Keep going for five breaths in and out, or as long as you like.

These children are having fun belly breathing! What did you put on your belly? Draw it on Mila's tummy!

Mila's tummy

Activity: Wiggle your toes

If you're feeling anxious, it can be hard to get your mind off those anxious thoughts. Worries spin around in your head, making your whole body feel tense. One trick to help with a busy, worrying brain that won't switch off is to focus your attention on the part of your body that's furthest away from your brain: your toes!

Try it:

✧ Think about your toes.

✧ Move them around a bit.

✧ If you can, take off your shoes and socks.

✧ Can you wiggle each toe, one at a time? Perhaps some are more difficult than others to wiggle.

✧ Can you scrunch up your toes, as if you're picking something up with them?

✧ Can you stretch them, so there's a big gap between each?

Activity: Powerful positive affirmations

Affirmations are short sentences that we can use to help remind us that we are safe, we are brave and we are not alone. When we say an affirmation to ourselves again and again, our brains get used to it and believe it more and more.

Everybody is different, so different affirmations will feel good for each person. Here's a whole tree full of affirmations – pick two or three that feel most calming to you.

Activity: Make your own affirmations

Which affirmations did you pick? You can choose from the tree or come up with your own. Write your three favourites on these leaves in big letters. You can colour and decorate the leaves too, if you like. When you're finished, carefully cut them out and stick them somewhere you'll see them every day – like your bedroom door or on the fridge.

Every time you see the statements, read them out loud and really believe they are true. It might feel strange at first, but in time it will help your bravery grow as strong as a tree.

Activity: Turn down the anxiety

Here's a fun way to shrink your worries using your imagination. Our brains are very powerful and sometimes imagining gives us the boost we need to shrink our worries.

Imagine this remote is in control of your emotions and thoughts. You can come back to this page, or imagine a remote control, whenever you want to take control of your thoughts and feelings.

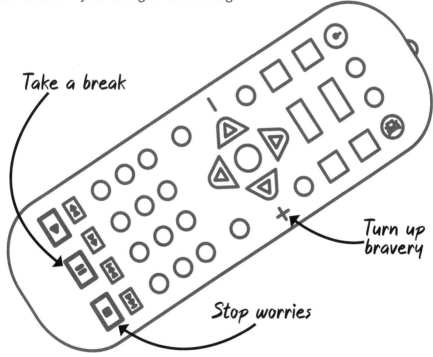

Take a break

Turn up bravery

Stop worries

Putting things into perspective

When you feel anxious, problems can feel absolutely ginormous! Worries about what to do or what will happen next feel like they're taking up your whole brain sometimes.

It can help to take a moment to work out the real size of your problem. If it's a really big problem, you'll probably need to find someone to help. But usually, problems aren't as big as they first feel – especially if you share them with a trusted grown-up.

First, write down your problem:

_____

What about this problem is worrying you?

_____

What's the next step you need to take to help solve the problem? Just pick one small thing you can do:

_____

Here are some ideas:
- Ask a grown-up for help
- Tell the truth
- Share your worry

When we think about problems as great big mountains, they feel scary and impossible to solve. But when we take a moment to work out what one small step we can take next, they shrink!

I am patient with myself

Activity: Calm colouring

Colouring is a wonderful way to feel calmer. Feel your anxiety shrink as your pen or pencil moves across the page.

The big wide world

Sometimes we hear about bad things that are happening in the world, and it can feel like the world is a big and frightening place. You might feel anxious about some of the things you learn about at school or in the news. It's important to remember that the news is made up of the bad, surprising or unusual things that happen in the world.

At any time, most of the seven billion people in the world are having normal days, a lot of people are having really good days and a few are having very bad days – we usually only hear about those few people having very bad days.

If the news was about all the good things that are happening in the world every single day, there wouldn't be time to get through them all!

If you feel scared or worried by the news or something going on in the world, remember that it's OK to switch off and take a break.

One brilliant way to feel better about the wider world is to make a positive difference in your town or neighbourhood. When you work with others to show kindness, bravery and generosity, you can change the world. If you see unfairness happening in your town, at school or somewhere else in the world, there is always something you can do to help.

It feels good to help others, and it helps shrink your worries and grow bravery when you realize what you can achieve. Even if it feels like you can only offer something small, those little good things add up and they inspire others to show kindness and bravery too!

Activity: Ripple effect experiment

Small things can make a big difference! Try this experiment to see how small actions spread.

You will need:

- ✦ A bowl or saucepan
- ✦ Cold water
- ✦ Four objects

How to:

1. Fill your bowl or saucepan with water.

2. Collect four objects from around your house, one of each kind: small, large, heavy, light.

3. One by one, drop the objects into the water and observe how they affect the water's surface.

Did you notice how even small or light objects create ripples that spread across the water's surface? When you do something kind for yourself, another person or the planet, you make an impact that spreads out.

Ripple effect scenario

On the way to school, Meena spotted some rubbish on the ground. She and her Mum carefully picked it up and put it in a nearby bin. It felt like a small thing, but here were its ripples:

 Because it was tidied away, an elderly man did not trip on the rubbish.

 Because it was not on the ground, a squirrel did not eat the rubbish and get ill.

 Someone on their way to work saw Meena and her Mum's kind act and felt inspired to do the same when they saw rubbish on the ground at the train station.

Worries shrink when you realize that you can always make a difference, even if it seems small. A kind word to yourself, asking for help or just taking a deep breath – little things are powerful.

Big fears

There are lots of things outside of our day-to-day lives that can make us feel scared and anxious, like storms, monsters or ghosts. Even if the chances of us experiencing these things is very small or even impossible, the idea of them can get stuck in our heads and cause us to worry.

If you're feeling this way, it's a good idea to sit down and confide in a trusted grown-up about the things that are worrying you. Your feelings matter and your grown-up will want to know if something is bothering or upsetting you.

When you're feeling calm and brave, you and your grown-up might like to find out all you can about the subject. This is a fun and interesting way to shrink your worries down to size.

Ask lots of questions, be curious and see if you can use knowledge to shrink your worries!

My feelings matter

Journalling out your worries

Lots of people like to write about their thoughts and feelings in a diary, journal or notebook. Writing about yourself and the things that frighten you helps take worries out of your mind and shrink them. All you need to start journalling is a notebook and a pen or pencil. Your journal can be just for you or, if you want to, you can show a trusted grown-up.

Try it out!

Use this space to write about how you are feeling and what is on your mind right now. Don't worry about spelling, grammar or being neat – and you can draw, too, if that feels good!

Take a moment to notice how it feels to journal. Has it helped you feel calmer or not made much difference? However journalling makes you feel is OK – you are the expert on what it's like to be you.

Thinking errors

Thinking errors are when your brain gets mixed up while trying very hard to keep you safe. The more times you have one of these thought mix-ups, the more you believe the thought is true. Let's learn about the different types of thinking errors.

FOCUSING ON THE NEGATIVES:
I got two questions wrong in my test – 8/10 isn't good enough.

ALL-OR-NOTHING THINKING:
If I fall off my new skateboard, I'm never getting on it again.

MAGNIFIED THINKING:
My trainers aren't very cool – nobody's going to want to be my friend.

MIND READING:
Everybody thinks I'm a bad person.

FORTUNE-TELLING:
All dogs will jump up and lick my face.

FEELINGS ARE FACTS:
I feel anxious about school today – that means something bad is going to happen.

PUTTING YOURSELF DOWN:
I'm useless, I shouldn't try.

UNREALISTIC EXPECTATIONS:
I should already be an expert gymnast.

BLAMING YOURSELF:
If I'd concentrated harder, my team would have won the maths competition.

Do any of these thought mix-ups sound like the voice you talk to yourself with? Colour in any that you recognize.

Remember, these kinds of thoughts are thinking errors and they are not true, just your brain getting mixed up while trying to keep you safe from negative experiences.

When you can recognize these mix-ups you can start to question them. The best idea is to talk them over with a trusted grown-up – quite often, talking about them can help you understand the mix-up better.

Thoughts, feelings and actions

How we think, how we feel and how we act are all linked. For example, Jackson feels anxious when there's a dog nearby. He thinks that if a dog comes near him, it will jump up and lick his face. If Jackson is visiting a friend's house and they have a pet dog, Jackson wants to leave, even if it's a small and well-behaved dog.

THOUGHT	FEELING	ACTION
All dogs will jump and lick	Afraid	Asks Mum to come and pick him up

Part 2: Shrinking worries

Everyone has different thoughts, feelings and actions. Here are some other ways people might think, feel and act when they see a dog at the park:

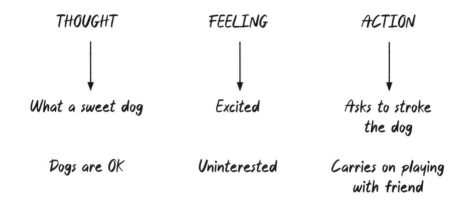

THOUGHT	FEELING	ACTION
What a sweet dog	Excited	Asks to stroke the dog
Dogs are OK	Uninterested	Carries on playing with friend

Can you remember a time you felt anxious? What did you **think**? What did you **feel**? What did you **do**?

THOUGHT	FEELING	ACTION

What's happening to make Jackson feel very anxious?

When Jackson was younger, an excited dog jumped up and licked his face. It felt scary and yucky, and Jackson was very upset. Jackson really, really doesn't want to feel that way again, so his brain makes a rule: stay away from all dogs, just in case.

The feeling of anxiety is Jackson's brain's way of making him feel very uncomfortable when a dog is nearby. Because he feels very anxious and uncomfortable, he wants to get far away from the dog as quickly as possible. So Jackson's brain has succeeded in its mission to keep Jackson safe from a dog jumping up and licking him.

The problem is, now Jackson misses out on playing at some of his friends' houses because they have dogs. Jackson feels disappointed and upset that his feeling of anxiety gets in the way of his plans.

What can Jackson do?

In order to shrink his worries, Jackson can start to think about his thoughts. Remember Jackson's thought on page 62? Jackson thought:

All dogs will jump and lick

Jackson can ask himself, is that 100 per cent true? The answer is: no! Not all dogs jump up and lick people's faces. So the thought "All dogs will jump and lick" is a thinking error.

Jackson is having a thought mix-up called "fortune-telling" – thinking he can see the future and thinking something bad will definitely happen!

It's tricky when you're feeling anxious, but when you think calmly and carefully, you realize that the thought is not true. Just because a dog jumped up at Jackson once, doesn't mean this will happen with every dog.

In this chapter we've been learning all about how our emotions affect our thoughts and actions, as well as clever ways to help ourselves feel calm. In the next chapter we're going to explore how we can use the power of our thoughts to shrink worries and grow bravery.

Part 3:
Growing bravery

Now we've learned all about worries and how to shrink them down to size, it's time to find out how to grow your bravery! In this chapter you'll find ideas and activities that will help you be kind to yourself, get curious about how you think, and learn ways to act with bravery and confidence.

Fact or opinion?

You're doing so brilliantly well! Let's build on what we've learned so far and find out more about how anxiety works.

Do you know the difference between a fact and an opinion? Facts are things that are always true, no matter what anyone says, thinks or wishes. Opinions are things we think or feel – someone else might think or feel differently. Here are some examples:

FACT:
Snow is cold
OPINION:
Winter is the best season

FACT:
We need to drink water in order to be healthy
OPINION:
Water tastes boring

FACT:
Horses can't fly
OPINION:
Zebras are better than horses

Activity: My fact file

What facts do you know? Fill in the gaps…

A fact about my face… (E.g. I have brown eyes.)

_____

A fact about my life… (E.g. My birthday is…)

_____

A fact about my home… (E.g. I have two bedrooms and one bathroom.)

_____

A fact about something I am interested in…
(E.g. Jupiter has more than 80 moons; a horse's height is measured in hands; red and yellow paint mixed together makes orange.)

_____

A fact about today… (E.g. I had toast and jam for breakfast.)

_____

Other facts I know… (E.g. The capital of Poland is Warsaw; 3x3=9; mayonnaise is made from eggs.)

_____

Part 3: Growing bravery

Now let's think about opinions – can you write some of your opinions in the gaps?

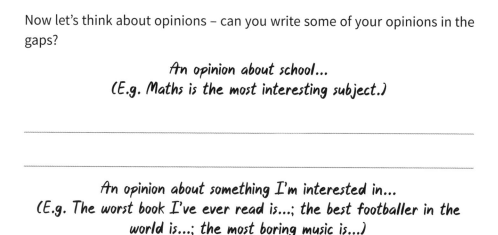

An opinion about school...
(E.g. Maths is the most interesting subject.)

_____

_____

An opinion about something I'm interested in...
(E.g. The worst book I've ever read is...; the best footballer in the world is...; the most boring music is...)

_____

_____

An opinion about today...
(E.g. Today was fun; my lunch was better than my best friend's lunch; it was silly when we had to miss 5 minutes of break time.)

_____

_____

Now we've thought about the difference between facts and opinions, let's find out how we can use this knowledge to shrink our worries!

Doing my best is best for me!

Thoughts aren't facts

As we learned on page 60, thinking errors are opinions that are pretending to be facts. If you feel anxious about something, it can feel very real and very true. It makes sense that you want to avoid the problem or situation that's causing you to worry to help you feel calmer and more comfortable.

But the key to shrinking your worries and growing bravery is understanding that anxious thoughts are just our brains trying their best to keep us safe in case something goes wrong. The problem is that our anxious thoughts can't know the future.

You can think that the sky is green or bananas are vegetables, but if you look around at the world, you will find that these thoughts aren't facts. You can think that all dogs will jump up and lick your face, or that you won't have a friend to sit next to at lunch, but thinking these thoughts does not make them more likely to happen.

When we learn to question our anxious thoughts, we can test them out. This is how we build bravery – by proving our anxious thoughts wrong. It can be scary to act with bravery when we're feeling very anxious.

Keep reading to learn about ways to make it feel easier.

What if...?

We've learned about how thoughts aren't facts and how thinking something bad will happen doesn't make it more likely to happen. But sometimes, bad things do happen. Often, our worries come from a tricky experience that we don't want to happen again – like when a dog jumped up at Jackson (see page 62).

Our brains can get so wrapped up with trying to stop it from happening that we forget how resilient we are. It's likely that you've had some challenges in your life – things that have felt really difficult. Even though it might have felt horrible at the time, you got through it and that's something to celebrate and feel proud of. Because you've overcome challenges already, you know you are strong enough to face new challenges.

When you let your brain think about what you would do if your worry came true, you can come up with an action plan. Here's an example from Ruby:

Ruby worries about getting lost when she goes to new places. She worries that she'll lose sight of her grown-up and they won't be able to find each other. This has never happened to Ruby but she can't get the worry out of her head. She doesn't like going to new places and tries to get her family to stay at home because she feels so anxious about it. Ruby tells her mum and dad how she feels, and they listen. They reassure Ruby that her feelings matter and they want to help her feel more comfortable. The family are planning a holiday in the summer and they want Ruby to have a calm and fun time. They decide to make a plan, just in case Ruby gets lost.

- ✧ Each time they go out, they'll all agree a meeting point in case they lose sight of each other
- ✧ Mum and Dad will make sure their phones are on loud

Part 3: Growing bravery

⭐ Ruby will carry their phone numbers and the address of where they are staying

⭐ If she gets lost, Ruby will ask a cafe or shop worker, or another grown-up with children for help

Having a plan in case her worry comes true helps Ruby feel braver about going on holiday. It would still feel scary to get lost, but now she and her parents know what to do to find each other again. Ruby's worry feels smaller now, and her bravery has grown.

SHRINK YOUR WORRIES

If you have a worry like Ruby, you could try making your own plan. Sit down with a trusted grown-up and talk about your worry, and make a plan just in case it happens. This will help you understand that you will be OK, even if your worry comes true.

☆ _____

_____

☆ _____

_____

☆ _____

_____

☆ _____

_____

Taking a moment to face our worries is brave. Bravery like this is what makes worries shrink. You're doing a great job!

Listening to our thoughts and feelings

Sometimes, when we feel anxious, it's hard to work out why we are feeling that way. Take a moment to listen to your body and pay attention to your thoughts.

✧ Where can you feel the anxiety in your body?

✧ What does it feel like?

✧ What thoughts, memories or images is your brain thinking about?

Once you've found out a bit more about your anxious thoughts and feelings, think about breaking them down into smaller pieces. Here's an example:

Lucas is feeling anxious in his chest. It feels tight and like he can't take a deep breath. He's imagining his teacher being angry with him. Lucas feels anxious because he can't find his library book and it's due back on Monday.

First, Lucas tells his grown-up how he's feeling. Together, they work out how to help Lucas feel calm and brave. Here's their plan:

✦ **Straight away:**

Lucas can do some breathing exercises to calm his mind and body

✦ **Later today:**

Lucas and his grown-up can look for the book together

✦ **Next time:**

They can come up with a safe place to keep library books so they're easier to keep track of

Why don't you have a go at writing or drawing some thoughts in the same way as Lucas?

✦ **Straight away:**

_____

✦ **Later today:**

_____

✦ **Next time:**

_____

I am resilient

Activity: Draw your anxious feeling

We learned about listening to our bodies, noticing where we feel anxiety and what it feels like. Now let's see if we can draw that feeling.

What does your anxious feeling look like? Can you draw or write about it below?

It could be a type of weather, monster, animal, person, robot or shape – use your imagination, you can even give it a name!

Drawing our big feelings helps us get to know them better, which builds our bravery!

Talk to your anxious feeling

Now you've drawn your anxious feeling, can you imagine yourself talking to it?

If you are feeling anxious, take a deep breath and let a calm feeling into your mind.

When you feel calm enough, you can ask your worry questions to find out the facts:

What are my worried thoughts and feelings trying to keep me safe from?

What am I thinking?

Are my thoughts facts or opinions?

Once you have taken the time to ask yourself these questions, you'll hopefully find that your bravery has grown. On the next page you'll see Isabella talk to her worry, so you can see how it's done.

Isabella's worry

Isabella is worried about being sick. Last Halloween, she got ill the same day she tried pumpkin soup. The doctor said it was a germ that made her sick, not the pumpkin, but she doesn't want to be near a pumpkin in case she gets ill again.

It's Halloween now and pumpkins are everywhere! She wants to go trick-or-treating with her friends but is worried about being close to pumpkins.

Now let's talk to that worry and look for some facts:

What are my worried thoughts and feelings trying to keep me safe from?
They are trying to keep me safe from being sick again.

What am I thinking?
If I get too near to a pumpkin it will make me sick again.

Are my thoughts facts or opinions?
Opinions – the doctor said it wasn't the pumpkin that made me ill, it was a germ.

Am I having a thought mix-up?
Yes – fortune-telling. I think if I stay away from pumpkins I'll never be sick again.

If my worry comes true, will I be OK?
Yes – it will feel horrid if I get ill, but I'll be OK.

What is the best thing that could happen?

I have a nice time trick-or-treating with my friends and don't get ill.

What will probably happen?

I might feel uncomfortable if I see a pumpkin, but I will be OK and still have a nice time. Like the doctor said, I probably won't get ill.

I can try new things

Be kind to yourself

When we learn about changing our thoughts and feelings, it can seem like we need to rush and make changes quickly, otherwise we're not doing it right. The truth is, everybody feels anxious and has thought mix-ups – even grown-ups. The way to make changes to how you think and feel is not to force, rush or hurry yourself. Instead, being kind and patient with yourself is the best way to feel better and braver.

When we're impatient or unkind to ourselves, we start to worry about worrying! Anxiety about whether we're thinking anxious thoughts just adds more worries to our minds.

You are OK just as you are. Shrinking your worries is not a race or something you should already know how to do – it's a skill we can learn just like any other.

Our minds and emotions grow with us – throughout your life there will always be something new to learn!

Activity: My self-love gloves

There are lots of things you can do to be kind to yourself and show yourself love. To help you think of what self-love and kindness means to you, design some self-love gloves! On this hand, you'll find things you can do to make yourself feel good.

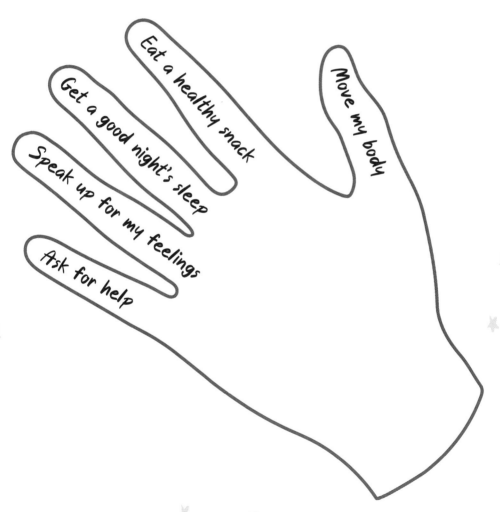

On this page, draw around your hand with a pencil and write five more things you can do to show yourself love and kindness. These might be things you enjoy doing, ways you can stick up for yourself or a favourite way to feel calm. Decorate your self-love gloves with bright colours and funky patterns!

I like being me!

Activity: I'm brave!

Now it's time to be really brave. Being brave isn't about never feeling afraid – true bravery means feeling scared, but facing our fears and doing it anyway. In the next few pages we're going to see how being brave can help you shrink your worries.

Can you think of a time you were really brave? Write or draw about it here:

What are anxious behaviours?

When we feel worried and think anxious thoughts, we try to do things to escape those anxious thoughts and feelings.

The trouble is, anxious behaviours don't shrink your worries – they make them grow bigger. By avoiding facing our fears, our worries grow and our bravery shrinks.

Here's an example to explain this idea further:

Umar has an appointment at the dentist. He feels very anxious about it – he can feel anxiety in his stomach and keeps thinking the dentist will do something that hurts him. He tells his carer that he's not feeling well, so he doesn't have to go to the dentist.

Skipping this appointment makes Umar's anxious thoughts and feelings go away for a little while, but when it's time to go again, it feels even more frightening to Umar. What should Umar do?

Going to the dentist feels really scary to Umar, but he knows that he needs to have his teeth checked. Umar decides to talk honestly to his carer about how he is feeling, and together they come up with a plan.

First, Umar asks his worry some questions to find out the facts.

What is my worry trying to keep me safe from? Feeling pain or discomfort at the dentist surgery

If my worry came true, would I be OK? It would feel bad, but my carer would keep me safe and the dentist would stop

What will probably happen? The dentist will check my teeth and won't need to do any painful treatments

Umar's bravery plan

Next, Umar and his carer make a plan to help build up Umar's bravery.

1. Read a book together about what happens at a dentist appointment.

2. Visit the dentist's office, just to look around.

3. Watch a YouTube video about what happens at a dentist appointment.

4. Umar comes along to his carer's dentist appointment.

5. Create a hand signal that means Umar wants to take a break.

6. Umar has a dentist appointment.

Umar plans to take small steps towards his goal, each time growing his bravery a little more. If it takes a while for Umar to be ready to take the next step, that's OK! Each step grows his bravery steadily until he feels ready to show the dentist his teeth.

I can do hard things

Activity: My bravery plan

Think about what makes you feel anxious. Can you design your own bravery plan to help grow your bravery steadily, one step at a time?

1. _____

2. _____

3. _____

4. _____

5. _____

6. _____

When things don't go as planned

When you're taking brave steps, mistakes and surprises come along – it's part of the adventure! When we make mistakes or things don't work out how we thought they would, it can feel really difficult and we worry about making that same mistake again.

But the truth is, every mistake contains a hidden gift. The key is to look closely…

Amelia is learning a new magic card trick. She's practised lots on her own and feels ready to try it out on her brother Felix.

But when she tries the trick with Felix, her trick doesn't work! She feels a bit embarrassed and less confident about herself.

Felix shows her the card he picked, and Amelia works out why she guessed a different one.

Amelia has learned so much more about the trick now, and realizes that by making a mistake she has worked out how to do it perfectly – this is her hidden gift. The next time she tries it, it works!

Activity: Celebrate you

Each brave step you take – however small it seems – is a big deal and worth celebrating. Bravery looks different on everybody, so others around you might not always understand quite how brave you are being.

Each time you take a brave, courageous step that shrinks your worries, even just a little bit, celebrate by adding it to one of the awards and trophies on this and the following page and colour it in.

Part 4: Shrink your friendship worries

Having friendships and meeting new people brings fun and fascination into our lives – but sometimes, it can also bring worries. Our fellow human beings have a big effect on our emotions and thoughts, so in this chapter we'll explore how to build great friendships that feel good.

True friendships

A true friendship is one where both friends feel relaxed together, they can talk and listen to each other about lots of things, and they're interested in getting to know and understand each other exactly as they are.

We can have all different levels of friendships, including true friends, best friends, people we like and those we are friendly with. Not everybody can be true friends with each other, because it takes time to build a true friendship.

Just because someone spends time with you and says they are your friend, it doesn't make it true! Sometimes, someone might say they're your friend but not act like a friend at all.

False friends are like bullies in disguise. Remember: you don't have to spend time with people who are unkind to you.

A True Friend	A False Friend
Listens to you	Ignores you
Talks to you kindly	Teases or embarrasses you
Stands up for you	Hurts you
Includes you	Leaves you out

I am
a good
friend

All about bullying

Bullying can happen in lots of different ways, and it can happen in real life or online. Often, bullies will make you feel like you deserve to be treated badly, which can make it hard to spot bullying.

Bullying can be:

- Hurting, embarrassing or upsetting you on purpose
- Taking your belongings without permission
- Making you do something you don't want to do
- Gossiping or telling lies about you
- Calling you names or teasing you
- Pushing and shoving
- Leaving you out
- Doing things on purpose that they know upset you

If you are being bullied, it's not your fault. Talk to a trusted grown-up about what is happening. You are important and you deserve to be treated with respect.

You are not alone

If you're being bullied, it can feel very lonely and like no one understands. Sometimes, it can even feel like we don't deserve good friends, or that there's no way out of the bullying. Even if you feel this way, you can talk to a trusted grown-up about what's happening to you. Talking to someone is the first step to shrinking bullies' power, and you are not alone.

Kindness and respect are for everybody

What do you worry about in friendships?

Every friendship is unique, so there can be lots of things that cause you to worry and feel anxious. Unkind words, a friend not showing up for school, wanting to make new friends… What friendship worries do you have? Write them here:

_____

_____

_____

_____

_____

Most friendship worries come from a fear that our friends will not want to spend time with us anymore and that we'll be alone. This is a very upsetting thought, and it's totally understandable that we can feel big emotions about friendships.

The very best thing to do if you are having trouble with a friendship worry is to talk to your friend and a trusted grown-up. It can feel scary to ask a friend if something is wrong, but without asking, our brains will fill in the gaps with worries.

Activity: Fill the gaps with facts!

Noor and Charlotte are best friends. They love chatting about anything and everything, and are always happy to see each other. Each Saturday, they go to the same gymnastics club and they learn brilliant new skills together.

One Saturday, Charlotte is on the way to gymnastics when her mum's car breaks down. They have to wait for the roadside rescue and Charlotte is so upset to miss gymnastics!

Meanwhile, at gymnastics, Noor is looking at the clock, wondering where Charlotte is. She begins to feel anxious, and her brain gets busy filling the gaps with worries:

Imagine you are Charlotte, what facts could you tell Noor to help shrink her worries?

_____

_____

Noor decides to talk to a trusted grown-up – her gymnastics teacher.

Can you see how talking about her feelings and getting some facts helped Noor shrink her worries?

Everyone has their own special way of being themselves

My friends gallery

Now we're reaching the end of the chapter, can you draw some of your friends in the gallery? You can include trusted grown-ups, relatives, babysitters, pets… whoever feels like a good friend to you!

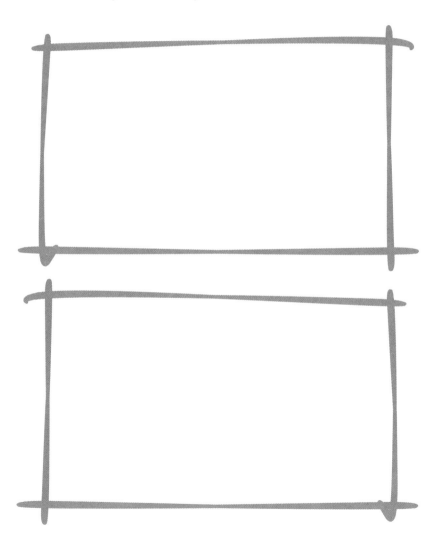

Part 5:
Taking care of you

Being brave and shrinking your worries is hard work and you should be really proud of yourself! We are at our strongest and bravest when our bodies feel good. When we've had enough sleep, drunk plenty of water and eaten well, our minds and bodies can be more relaxed and being brave gets that much easier.

In this chapter we'll explore all the ways we can take great care of ourselves and treat ourselves with kindness so we can do our very best each day.

Time to chill out

When we relax, our breathing slows, our heartrate decreases and our muscles loosen. Simply by taking time to chill, we can reduce feelings of anxiety by quite a lot. Because anxious feelings often come with anxious thoughts, it helps to do something relaxing that our minds can focus on, rather than just chilling out with nothing to do.

Here are some ideas for relaxing activities that will help calm your body and shrink your worries:

- Find a piece of fruit and draw or paint a picture of it
- Rearrange your bookshelf by spine colour
- Lie on your bed and stretch your whole body
- Do a word or number puzzle
- Cook something with a parent or carer
- Go for a bike ride with a parent or carer
- Do some colouring
- Listen to some music
- Watch clouds in the sky – what shapes can you spot?
- Think about how your body feels from the top of your head to the tips of your toes
- Look out of the window and notice the details you don't usually see

Part 5: Taking care of you

Can you think of some more? Write or draw some of your own ideas here:

Spend time offline

Watching TV and playing online games is fun. No one likes feeling bored and having screens around means there's always something to entertain us. When we're feeling anxious, games, apps and TV shows can be a quick way to switch off from our thoughts and feelings.

The only problem is that super exciting things that distract us from our anxious thoughts and feelings don't help us actually deal with those thoughts and feelings.

It's OK to enjoy using screens and devices – they can be fun, relaxing, creative and you can learn lots of interesting things. But our brains and bodies need time off from being entertained, so that we can feel our feelings, express our thoughts and get to know ourselves better.

Chat with your grown-up about getting a good balance when it comes to screen time.

Scrunchy face experiment

When we feel anxious or upset, the muscles in our bodies become tense. We can feel more relaxed by noticing this feeling and taking a moment to release the tension from our bodies. Try this experiment and see what happens:

1. First, think about how relaxed you feel right now – give yourself a relaxation percentage and colour it on the bar.

2. Scrunch up your face, so your nose is wrinkled, your teeth push together and lines appear between your eyebrows.

3. Now relax and let your face go back to normal.

4. Give yourself another relaxation percentage – you can colour in the relaxation bar here:

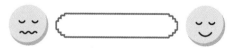

Did you feel your whole body relax when you relaxed your face muscles? When your face was scrunched up, your face muscles filled with tension. When you let it go back to normal, those muscles relaxed. Relaxing one part of your body helps your whole body relax.

Activity: Body movement breathing

Taking a big, deep breath is a great way to make yourself feel that bit calmer and braver any time. Body movement breathing will help you take really deep breaths, filling your body with oxygen and energy.

1. First, stand on the floor with socks or bare feet.

2. Breathe in and reach up to the ceiling, spreading your arms wide.

3. Breathe out and let your body flop forward and down, so your arms hang in front of your legs.

4. Stand up straight and repeat for five breaths in and out.

I am kind to myself

You are the best and there is only one of you

Some people think that the way we look is important. Every day we see people on TV and online looking a bit like regular people but somehow shinier and neater. But did you know, that's not how those people look in real life? Special lights on TV and effects on photographs mean that normal human beings can be made to look like aliens from Planet Perfect!

Worrying about how we or other people look is a waste of time. Nobody exists just for other people to look at – we exist to learn, grow and find out what makes us happy. There are a million more interesting things to do and think about other than how we look, and you're already the best and only version of you in the entire universe.

Next time you look in the mirror, tell yourself you're awesome!

Activity: Make a nature mandala

A mandala is a symmetrical, circular pattern. Mandalas were invented by Buddhist and Hindu teachers as a way to help them meditate and focus their minds.

You can make a mandala using natural objects you find in your garden, during a walk through the woods or a trip to the beach. Here's a nature mandala you can colour in right now!

It's a good idea to make your mandala in the same place you find your natural objects. This way, you can have fun creating the mandala and then let the natural objects go back into their environment. Don't forget to take a picture – or even better, sketch your nature mandala on this page!

Does water help shrink worries?

We know the water in a washing machine can shrink a woolly jumper, but can drinking a glass of water really shrink our worries? Scientists say yes!

The amount of water in our bodies has a big effect on how our brains work, our energy levels and the emotions we feel. This is because we need water for almost everything our bodies do. When we have even a little bit less water than we need, it makes us feel tired, stressed out and poorly.

A glass of water can help you feel more relaxed and energized when you're having a hard time with anxiety.

While plain water is the best thing to drink for our bodies, it can be a bit boring. Here are some ideas for making water more fun:

✧ Add cucumber, lemon or lime slices

✧ Get a cool water bottle or loopy straw

✧ Try fizzy water instead

Did you know?

You can check whether you're drinking enough water by looking at the colour of your wee. If it's pale yellow, you're drinking enough. If it's darker, it's time for a drink!

Body worries

Our bodies are amazing – and often a little annoying! Feelings of anxiety, aches and pains, wishing we could run faster or be a little bit taller… everybody has feelings of frustration about their bodies sometimes.

If you have a worry about your body, write or draw it here:

Can you think of three things you're grateful to your body for? E.g. My back for learning how to do a backflip; my eyes for reading this book; my fingers for drawing.

⭐ _____

⭐ _____

⭐ _____

Your body naturally changes as you get older and start to grow into an adult, which might make you feel worried or embarrassed. Remember these changes are normal and they happen to everyone.

It's common to feel shy about your body, and remember that no one but you is allowed to see or touch your body without your permission. You can always talk to a trusted grown-up about anything to do with your body that's worrying or confusing you.

Eat well, feel calm

When we eat food that's good for our bodies and we love the taste of, we naturally feel good! Healthy food brings nutrients, vitamins and minerals to our bodies that keep us feeling calm and energized.

Cooking can be a relaxing activity – creating something delicious for your family to eat is a wonderful way to boost your confidence. Why not try this simple home-made pasta recipe?

You will need:

✧ 100 g (3½ oz) plain flour per person

✧ One egg per person

✧ Water

How to:

1. Tip the flour onto a board and use your fingers to make a dip in the centre.

2. Carefully crack the egg into the dip and use a fork to break the yolk.

3. With your hands, slowly mix the flour into the egg. When all the egg is absorbed, you can add a bit of water if needed or another egg.

4. Keep slowly bringing the flour into the egg mixture until there are no dry bits of flour left.

5. Knead (press, fold and massage with your hands) the dough for 10 minutes. If it feels sticky, add a little flour. If it feels dry, add a drop of water.

6. Now wrap the dough in clingfilm or a beeswax wrap and leave it alone for 30 minutes.

7. Sprinkle flour onto your board and use a rolling pin to roll the pasta dough really flat. It's easier if you break the dough into lumps and roll them out one at a time.

8. When your dough is as thin as you can get it – ideally 2–3 mm (⅛ in.) thick – use a butter knife to cut it into shapes. Long, flat ribbons are yummy, but you can use your imagination.

9. Get a grown-up to help you bring a pan of salted water to the boil.

10. Carefully add your pasta shapes to the boiling water and let them cook for 2 minutes.

11. Ask a grown-up to drain the pasta and serve with your favourite pasta sauce!

Did you know?

Kneading and rolling have a calming effect on our minds and bodies, helping to shrink worries!

Activity: Time to dream

Getting plenty of sleep will help you feel calmer, happier and give you more energy during the day. Sleep gives your brain time to work out everything that has happened to you or been on your mind during the daytime. Often problems that are bugging you during the day can seem a lot more manageable after a good night's sleep!

Worries and feelings of anxiety can make it very difficult to fall asleep. Talking to a trusted grown-up about what's on your mind can help shrink your worries enough so you can go to sleep.

Here's another trick for when worries are keeping you awake, it's called "Child's Pose" and it's a special yoga stretch for helping you feel safe and calm.

Tuck your feet under your bottom and stretch forward on your bed, so your forehead touches your pillow and your arms are stretched out in front of you. Feel the lovely stretch along your back and arms, and breathe deeply. You can stay in Child's Pose for as long as you want to. Notice how it makes you feel calmer and sleepier.

It's cool to be me

Part 6:
Looking to the future

We're nearly at the end of this book! Hopefully you've found out some interesting new ideas and skills for shrinking your worries and understanding your thoughts and emotions. In this chapter we'll learn how to put your new skills into practice.

Activity: Take a moment

Taking a moment to stop and think about how you feel and the ways in which you're lucky is a brilliant way to shrink your worries and feel calm. On the next few pages you'll find lots of space to write or draw about what it's like to be you, in this very moment.

Can you list ten things you're grateful for today? They can be big or small: E.g. a bird singing; a funny movie; a trip you're looking forward to.

Part 6: Looking to the future

What's something that feels tricky right now? E.g. a friendship worry.

How are you being kind to yourself while you deal with this challenge?

E.g. I am talking to my trusted grown-up about how I feel.

Part 6: Looking to the future

The best part of today was...

Challenges help me grow and learn

Activity: Shrink your worries cheat sheet

You've learned so much about anxiety, worries, thoughts and feelings! Here's a cheat sheet with some of the most important ideas and tools from this book. When you want to shrink your worries in a hurry, turn to this page!

Talk to a trusted grown-up

Look for facts

Take some deep breaths

Is my brain having a thinking error?

Remember that it's OK to feel how you are feeling

Move your body

Try a positive affirmation like "I am safe"

Wiggle your toes!

Do some colouring or doodling

Show kindness to yourself and others

Write down your worries

Listen: what are you thinking, feeling and doing?

Break it down into brave steps

I can grow my bravery!

Activity: My top tips for shrinking worries

Now you've learned all about shrinking your worries, what are your top tips? They might be from this book, something you've come up with yourself or something you've been told about.

Write your top tips here:

_____

_____

_____

_____

_____

_____

_____

_____

Farewell

You've reached the end of *Shrink Your Worries* – well done! You've learned some incredible things, and it makes sense if it all feels like quite a lot of information. You can go back and read this book again, or skip to the part you're interested in at any time.

You are brave, brilliant and capable of overcoming challenges. You are becoming a wonderful friend to yourself, which will help you through life's ups and downs. Every day you are growing your bravery and kindness, and the world is lucky to have you in it.

I can shrink my worries

For parents and carers: Helping your child deal with anxious thoughts and feelings

When your child is showing signs of anxiety, it can be so difficult to know what to do. We want our children to feel happy, calm and confident and it's upsetting to see them struggling. It's important to remember that feelings of anxiety are normal and that struggles can present an opportunity to learn new skills and gain new experiences – even if it feels horrible at the time.

If you've looked through this book, you'll see that talking to a trusted grown-up is mentioned often. If you show your child patience and a willingness to understand what it's like to be them, you will be a trusted grown-up to them. If you notice something's not quite right, don't be afraid to ask them and start a conversation about how they're feeling.

Reassuring them that we all sometimes feel down or anxious without an obvious cause can be a great way to open a conversation, as it takes away any pressure they may feel to explain their emotions.

Let go of any pressure you yourself feel to say the perfect thing – it doesn't exist. On the contrary, being imperfect and doing your best anyway will demonstrate to your child that they don't need to be perfect either. Healthy strong relationships with parents and carers help create resilient kids, because within these relationships everyone is able to be themselves and feel accepted.

Sometimes, your child will come to you with a problem they need help solving. But more often, they will simply be looking for a listening ear. The power of a parent or carer showing acceptance and understanding for their child's feelings should not be underestimated – the old saying "a problem shared is a problem halved" is absolutely true.

If their worries get overwhelming and your child is panicking and acting out, remember this is their brain telling them that they might be in danger

– they aren't being difficult, naughty or manipulative. To help them deal with overwhelming feelings, you can:

- Make sure you are both somewhere safe

- Come down to their level and take some deep breaths together

- Do your best to name their feelings: "You're feeling scared/angry/nervous"

- Hold their hand if they want you to

- Walk or sway with them, if it feels right

- Stay calm, stay with them and show them that you are not overwhelmed by their emotions

It can feel very, very stressful when your child is struggling and overwhelmed. Once they feel calm again, take some time to calm yourself. Staying present with a child's big emotions is an act of great love and courage, and it often involves putting our own feelings to the side. Be kind to yourself and take some deep breaths, talk to a friend, or whatever you need to care for yourself.

It's natural for loving parents to want to shield their children from negative feelings, whether it's from friendship worries, phobias or stressful life events. But avoiding things that make your child anxious only gives a short-term benefit, and giving children the space and time to talk about and understand their feelings is what will help carry them through tough times.

When it comes to big life changes like a house move, new school, bereavement or divorce, talk to your child early and in an age-appropriate way. Take each conversation as it comes and allow your child to express their feelings. The more they feel comfortable expressing difficult emotions without judgement or pressure, the more these feelings will evolve and the easier it will be for your child to accept the change or challenge they are facing.

Finally, let go of guilt – it's tempting to blame ourselves for our children's struggles, or to try and make life as easy as we can for them.

By metaphorically (and sometimes literally) holding their hand as they face life's challenges, you are helping them build the resilience, emotional intelligence and courage they'll need later in life. Often, when our children come to us with a worry or problem, the most powerful thing we can offer them is love and understanding, rather than a solution – teaching them that as long as we are being a good friend to ourselves, no problem is insurmountable.

Further advice

Anxiety doesn't feel nice, but it is normal. If you have serious concerns about how your child's thoughts and feelings are affecting their life and mental health, it's best to start by talking to your doctor and your child's school. The following organizations also offer advice, information and support:

YoungMinds' free parent helpline:
0808 802 5544

Mind:
www.mind.org.uk
0300 123 3393
info@mind.org.uk

Childline:
www.childline.org.uk
0800 1111

NHS Choices:
www.nhs.uk/mental-health

BBC Bitesize Parents' toolkit:
www.bbc.co.uk/bitesize/parents

Child Mind Institute (USA):
www.childmind.org

Mental Health America:
www.mhanational.org

Recommended reading

For kids:
A Handful of Quiet
Thích Nhất Hạnh

Healthy, Happy Minds
The School of Life

Wreck This Journal
Keri Smith

For adults:
Good Inside
Dr Becky Kennedy

The Book You Wish Your Parents Had Read
Philippa Perry

The Story Cure
Ella Berthoud and Susan Elderkin

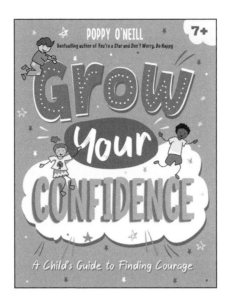

Grow Your Confidence

978-1-83799-171-6

A mood-boosting, confidence-building companion to help 7+-year-olds become their happiest selves

Confidence is something many people struggle with throughout their lives. Supporting children as they face this challenge can help them grow into self-assured, happy individuals.

Encourage your child to explore their emotions, overcome their fears and boost their self-confidence with this positive and playful book. Bursting with fun activities, handy tips and simple exercises, *Grow Your Confidence* is the go-to guide to help children feel good about who they are.

Calm-a-Doodle

978-1-83799-214-0

It's time to chill out with this supersized, super-cool doodling and colouring extravaganza!

Take a breather, get comfy and grab your colouring pens and pencils. This activity book offers plenty of beautiful illustrations and patterns to colour, along with starter doodles to help your imagination flow and your worries float away. Inspired by techniques used by psychologists to help children cope with difficult feelings through mindfulness, this delightful doodle book is the perfect tool to help you find calm while also having lots of fun.

My Emotions and Me

978-1-80007-994-6

A stunning and playful graphic novel exploring emotions and how to cope with them, for everyone from 7 to 107!

Did you know:
- When you're experiencing a feeling, it's much easier to feel the emotion rather than put it into words?
- The four basic emotions – anger, joy, sadness and fear – all have a positive function?
- You can ease intense feelings by inviting them into your body, and with some deep breathing you can feel calm again?

Join Art-mella and her furry sidekick Rattie as they go on a fascinating voyage of self-discovery where they learn all about emotions; why we have them, how we process them and techniques on how to cope with them.

Have you enjoyed this book?
If so, why not write a review on your favourite website?

If you're interested in finding out more about our books,
find us on Facebook at **Summersdale Publishers**,
on Twitter/X at **@Summersdale** and on Instagram and
TikTok at **@summersdalebooks** and get in touch.
We'd love to hear from you!

Thanks very much for buying this Summersdale book.

www.summersdale.com

Image Credits